# *SPEAKING OUR TRUTH* TEACHER GUIDE

by Tasha Henry

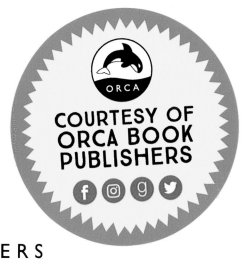

ORCA BOOK PUBLISHERS

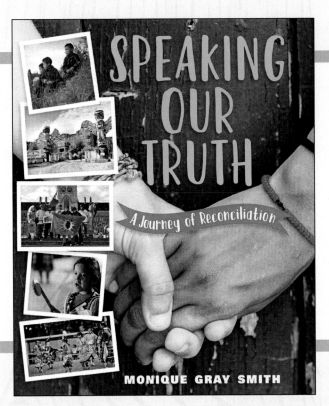

**This is the companion teacher guide to**
***Speaking Our Truth:***
***A Journey of Reconciliation***
Monique Gray Smith

9781459815834 HC
Ages 9–12
speakingourtruth.ca

★ "Replete with primary sources, including photos and personal accounts from those who lived in the Residential Schools, Smith tackles difficult and complex conversations with straightforwardness and compassion...Despite the somber topic, Smith consistently empowers readers to be agents of change and provides specific suggestions to take action...Purchase this vibrant, must-have title to prompt critical thinking and open discussions."
—*School Library Journal*, starred review

Copyright © 2018 Tasha Henry

All rights reserved.

Orca Book Publishers gratefully acknowledges the support for its publishing programs provided by the following agencies: the Government of Canada, the Canada Council for the Arts and the Province of British Columbia through the BC Arts Council and the Book Publishing Tax Credit.

ORCA BOOK PUBLISHERS
orcabook.com

Printed and bound in the United States.

21  20  19  18  •  4  3  2  1

The URLs in this guide were working links at the time of publication. Orca Book Publishers has no control over their accuracy or continuing existence. They are included in good faith to provide users with additional information of potential interest.

# CONTENTS

# INTRODUCTION

## "Reconciliation begins with you."
—Dr. Robert Joseph, Gwawaenuk First Nation

For more than 150 years Indigenous children across Canada were forcibly taken from their homes and placed in Residential Schools, sometimes thousands of kilometers away from their communities. The youngest kids were just four or five years old. It's hard to imagine that happening in Canada today. But the last Residential School closed in 1996—not that long ago.

The sad and often tragic legacy of that time is still being felt by Survivors, their families and their communities. The journey to reconciliation with Canada's First Nations, Métis and Inuit peoples is only just beginning.

The Anishinaabe people have Seven Sacred Teachings. They are Honesty, Respect, Love, Courage, Truth, Humility and Wisdom. In Monique Gray Smith's book *Speaking Our Truth: A Journey of Reconciliation*, these teachings are a guide to understanding Canada's colonial history and the complex relationship between Indigenous and non-Indigenous people. They are also a path to reconciliation, a way to share a message of resilience and hope. Every Canadian, especially young people, can come on the journey and imagine a future where all kids can live free from discrimination.

"I welcome you all to the journey. In my *Nihiyaw* (Cree) language, we say *tawâw*, which loosely means 'there's always room.' For you, for me, for your friends, your family, your community. There's always room."
—Monique Gray Smith, author of *Speaking Our Truth*

## ABOUT THIS GUIDE

Welcome to the teacher guide for *Speaking Our Truth: A Journey of Reconciliation*. The guide follows the book, chapter by chapter, making it easy for teachers and students to dig deeper into the text and make personal connections to the material. Each chapter of the guide features a summary, essential questions, metaphors for learning, key concepts and vocabulary and detailed learning activities. There is bonus material about making art, keeping a journal and doing research. Activities are laid out clearly, with instructions for teachers and for students as they embark together on the journey of reconciliation.

SHARI NAKAGAWA

Interviews with a range of people, including school-age children, Indigenous Elders and Canada's Truth and Reconciliation commissioners, convey the multivoiced perspective that is essential for any process of reconciliation. Monique speaks directly to her young readers. The chapters are laid out as invitations to join a growing conversation that must be based on kindness and reciprocity as the first protocol of any social change. Welcome to the journey! We need you!

## A Call to Teaching

As educators, we are often called to teach beyond what we know or what we have experienced ourselves. This is the call of teaching, to learn *with* our students and have them shape the learning outcomes. Teaching about Canada's historic commitment to the Residential School system is a difficult yet imperative journey. So feeling *unsettled* or challenged by the content of this curriculum is exactly where we need to be to start the work of repairing colonialism's legacy through education. But where could this work lead us?

Dr. Marie Wilson reminds us in chapter four of *Speaking Our Truth* that it is the children who will "lead the way" and instruct us as to what dispositions and attitudes should be reflected in our practices and policies. As a teacher, then, your job is to be open to what emerges through your students' developing understanding of what Indigenous and non-Indigenous relationships could look like in this time of reconciliation. Holding open a space for your students, allowing emotions to be a part of the reflective process and allowing them to ask the hard questions is the pedagogy that Monique's book seeks. Part of responding to this call

TASHA HENRY

is to hold off on the desire for immediate answers or solutions to the questions presented in the chapters. This work is about allowing your students to imagine the types of societal structures that value justice, cultural diversity and equity.

And so, with Monique's suggestion to "think with your heart," view this teaching resource as an opportunity to join a curriculum that demands a personal journey, led by the work and vision of your students.

Thank you for joining us!

# Packing for Your Journey
*Teacher Checklist*

✓ Have you consulted with the First Nations in your area? Ask the simple question: "Given my learners, how should I proceed with this unit?"

✓ Create out-trips to the Nations, art galleries, reconciliation public events and exhibits, archeological sites/walks or local events celebrating First Nations, Métis and Inuit cultures and traditional languages. Most important, get to the land. Study the history through the forests, shrubs, rivers, lakes, prairies and oceans. What flora and fauna are Indigenous? What are the pre-contact stories that narrate the First Peoples' connections to land?

 ✓ Send out an information letter to your students' parents. Can your Aboriginal Student Support staff edit it accordingly? (See Handout #1.)

✓ How will you leave a message of hope, resiliency and positive self-esteem for your learners?

✓ If you are connecting with local artists and cultural workers, how are you modeling the simple acknowledgment of asking permission to study their stories, art and artifacts? Consider this short video about Indigenous arts protocols to get started: http://nationtalk.ca/story/indigenous-arts-protocols.

✓ How will you adapt the curriculum to make sure you are not retraumatizing intergenerational Residential School Survivors and their families?

# Ongoing Collaborative Learning Practices
## 1. Keep a "Reflection Journal"

Use the Reflection Questions (signified by the drum) in each chapter as springboard questions that invite sensitive discussions. Save fifteen minutes at the end of each lesson for silent writing, reflecting and drawing. Have your students identify how this book is different than others. Monique is speaking directly to them. If writing reflections in response to the questions feels hard, suggest that your students try starting each entry with *Dear Monique.*

Once a week, have your students pick their favourite journal entry and record it on a video camera or a cell phone. Use the prompt "It matters to me because…" Can you keep a video camera in the classroom and let students be in charge of recording and collating their reflections independently? As a culminating gesture, consider uploading selected edited responses to the TRC website page "It Matters to Me" (trc.ca/websites/reconciliation/index.php?p=328).

## 2. Work with Your Hands

Invite an Indigenous artist, Elder or willing family member into your classroom to share a cultural practice such as weaving, beading, drawing, sewing, cooking, carving, listening and speaking. Having your students work with their hands each day allows them to absorb and interpret difficult content. Please review this protocol if inviting a Residential School Survivor into your classroom: http://projectofheart.ca/step-4-survivor-visit.

TASHA HENRY

**Example:** I was honoured to have Mohawk/Iroquois artist Lindsay Delaronde teach our fifth- and sixth-grade students how to bead on leather and make moccasins. As we studied the history of colonization and Residential Schools, the students made their own **memory bags**. At the end of the unit, we placed our memory bags so they faced the traditional burial grounds of the Songhees people.

## 3. Make Art

Art is a great way to analyze, synthesize and represent knowledge. Choose a medium that can be part of your daily classroom practice. Work toward displaying your work as a temporary installation at your local art gallery, museum, community center or city hall. Have the children decide how they want to create their art intervention as a gesture toward reconciliation.

**Example:** As a culminating activity for their Reconciliation Studies unit, our grades three and four classes drew Coast Salish-inspired images on porcelain plates that I'd bought at a secondhand store. With the guidance and presence of Songhees carver and Elder Butch Dick, the children made an art installation

TASHA HENRY

with their plates in the main room of the Art Gallery of Greater Victoria. This was a response to the *Call to Action* to honour the unaccounted-for children who disappeared from Residential Schools. aggv.ca/learn/partner-school-inquiry

### 4. Find Your Words

Explore poetry writing, speech writing, spoken-word performance and song lyrics as mediums when responding to the content. Develop a portfolio experimenting with different forms of writing/speaking. Celebrate the work by having students select each other's work to create a *Reconciliation Anthology* with an editor's statement at the front and photos of student-created artwork. Or your students could host a spoken-word event and invite the community.

### 5. Create a Classroom Blog or Video

Use the Reflection Questions in each chapter to create video responses. Record interviews, reflections, photos, footage and music that explore some of the central concepts raised in the book. Collaborate with your local First Nations. Invite a class living on a reserve to collaborate via Skype. Submit your work to the National Centre for Truth and Reconciliation as an example of how to engage in classroom-based work.

## Daily Strategies for Meaningful Learning

- **Use Entrance and Exit Slips** to open and close each lesson (see Handout #2). Large sticky notes work well. Students can glue these in their reflection journals or hand them in so you can assess how they are processing the content and pace of your lessons.

- **Create a Learning Grid** where students input the different learning activities. Make sure your grid is multi-dimensional, demonstrating varied literacies and balancing the oral, written and digital (see Handout #3). Use the grid as a "study guide" at the end of the unit to review the scope of learning activities. Or have students pick one part of the grid as the basis for an Inquiry Project.

TASHA HENRY

- **Use a Talking Stick** to promote the quality of listening, speaking and respectful group discussion in your classroom. Use a musical instrument such as a rain stick or a bell to signify that it is time to listen and not speak. Turn your lights off to cue your students that it is time to reflect quietly.

- **Get outside.** I've taught in everything from big inner-city high schools to small alternative schools in portables. There is always a connection to be made through a relationship to the natural world. All you need is a cell phone, or paper and pencil, the right clothes and the willingness to see your environment differently.

# CHAPTER ONE—WELCOME TO THE JOURNEY

## Summary

This chapter introduces students to the history of Indigenous and settler relations in Canada, to Residential Schools, and to the Truth and Reconciliation Commission of Canada (TRC). The teachings are offered through the metaphor of a journey inward, where the Seven Sacred Teachings become the map for learning and healing a traumatic past.

*Metaphors for Learning about Reconciliation:* Medicine, healing, sweetgrass strands, purifying

*The Seven Sacred Teachings (Dispositions for Learning):* Honesty, Respect, Love, Courage, Truth, Humility, Wisdom

## Essential Questions

- Why do we need to go on a journey of reconciliation?
- What attitudes do we need to go on this journey?
- What attitudes are not welcome on this journey?

## Key Concepts and Vocabulary

Indigenous
racism: internalized and systemic
colonization
Indian agent
reconciliation
trauma
ally
Elders
Traditional Knowledge Keepers
oral traditions

## Learning Activity: Holding Each Other Up
*Teacher Instructions*

1. **Open the lesson** with the class sitting in a circle on the floor or on the grass outside, cross-legged, arms linked. Without talking, try to stand up as a circle without breaking the links. After trying a few times, ask the students what they learned about trying to stand up as a group.

2. **Think:** Use a **Word Splash** to explore the Reflection Questions on page 14. Have students brainstorm their previous knowledge in a mind map. Discuss their findings as a whole group. Read "Monique's Journey" on page 16. Why do you think she feels it is important to share her story?

3. **Essential Questions:**
   • Where are you situated?
   • On whose land do you reside?
   • Where were you born?
   • Are you of settler or First Peoples' ancestry?

*Student Instructions*

1. **Research** the traditional territory, language and history of the First Peoples on whose land you reside. Research the history of land negotiations. Divide into groups, choosing one topic each, and create a **Word Wall** with everything you have learned in your research. Include maps and visuals. Post the work on the classroom wall.

2. **Write** a territory acknowledgment in child-friendly language that would be used at assemblies and gatherings at your school. As a class, **develop criteria** for an introductory letter that would ask your school administration for permission to invite an Elder or cultural worker from a local First Nation to be a guest in your class. What protocols are expected by the Elders from this First Nation? What kinds of questions honour this protocol?

3. **Write** a proposal letter as a class. **Present it orally** to your principal, along with the territory acknowledgment. Here is a sample letter:

*Dear Administrative Team,*

*As you know, the Grade 7 class is starting a unit on Indigenous ways of knowing, Residential Schooling and Reconciliation. We would like to make this unit authentic and honour our Elders from the Songhees Nation. As you know, our school sits on unceded territory of the Lekwungen–speaking peoples, now known as the Songhees and Esquimalt Nations.*

*To open our unit, with respect to the Songhees protocol, we would like to invite an Elder to come to our classroom to share some teachings with us around Indigenous ways of learning and knowing.*

*As part of the required respect and protocol when interacting with Elders from our local Nations, we will need permission to pick him/her up, introduce him/her to our administration and staff with a proper territory acknowledgment and provide a hand-made gift from us. We would need to offer a monetary gift as well, which we would be happy to raise in a bake sale. We would then provide him/her with transport home before the end of the school day.*

*We hope you will see how valuable it is for us to open this unit of study with the presence of a member from the Songhees Nation.*

*Hay'sxw'qa si'em nakwilia*
*(Thank you, my honourable people),*
*The Grade 7 class*

(This assignment was adapted from the *edX* free course for educators "Reconciliation Through Indigenous Education.")

4. **Make art.** Instructions to students: Make a seven-strand braid using sweet-grass, long grass, ribbon or yarn. Draw a picture of the braid and label each strand with an example from your own life that represents one of the Seven Sacred Teachings. Each teaching should be illustrated by a personal experience, example or action. Tie the braids together to make one long braid or display them separately with the Seven Sacred Teachings graphic response.

5. **Close the lesson** with a discussion of the "Look After Yourself" suggestions on page 31. Discuss the importance of self-care when learning about and listening to traumatic events in history. Or close the lesson with a **One-Minute Exit Slip**. Have each student take one minute to write on a sticky note a feeling, question or thought that jumps out for them.

6. **Before starting the next lesson**, have each student complete an **Entrance Slip** (a sticky note with a question, thought, feeling or comment).

# CHAPTER TWO—HONESTY: WHERE HAVE WE COME FROM?

## Summary

This chapter explores the history of Canada's relationship with its First Peoples. The concepts of cultural genocide and cultural resiliency are examined through primary and secondary documents and the testimonies of Survivors and their families. The effects of colonialism are viewed through the lens of resiliency and hope.

## Key Concepts and Vocabulary

First Peoples
resiliency
Confederation
Indian Act
matriarchal
matrilineal
Indian status
potlatch
assimilation
sterilization
moral courage
intergenerational Survivor
Métis
Inuit

The words on the blackboard read *Thou Shalt Not Tell Lies.* LAC PA134110

*Entrance Slip:* Which of the Seven Sacred Teachings do you honour today as we enter into these lessons together, and why?

## Essential Questions

- How does colonization serve certain cultural groups?
- How do stereotypical images and ideas support the enterprise of colonization?
- How have colonialism and imperialism affected Indigenous and non-Indigenous identities and relations within Canada?

## Learning Activity: Analyzing Stereotypes

1. **Create a Contract.** Initiate a positive tone by creating a classroom contract. Have the students define which attitudes or beliefs are not welcome in the

classroom when learning about Canada's past and present relations with First Peoples. Flip negative language into positive. If they identify *racist comments* as a negative, what is the opposite? Inclusive comments? Post the contract and have each individual sign it. In future discussions, revisit the contract by randomly praising comments that promote positive interactions.

2. **Analyze Stereotypes.** Find old library books, textbooks or images that depict first contact between Canada's First Peoples and the European settlers.

3. **Watch** *I'm Not the Indian You Had in Mind* by Thomas King (nsi-canada.ca/2012/03/im-not-the-indian-you-had-in-mind/#) and print out the poem: facinghistory.org/stolen-lives-indigenous-peoples-canada-and-indian-residential-schools/chapter-2/i-m-not-indian-you-had-mind.

4. **Read** Helen Knott's article "The Indigenous people I read about as a kid were nothing like me—so I became a writer": chatelaine.com/living/indigenous-representation-literature.

5. **Questions for Discussion:**
   - How are stereotypes connected to racism?
   - How does the poem use sarcasm and irony to make you think about cultural representation? How would stereotypical images of First Peoples support the Indian Act?
   - How did stereotypes fuel the concept of assimilation?
   - How is the video, or Helen's article, effective in challenging these stereotypes? Who is Helen writing to/for?

## Learning Activity: Story Mapping

1. **Share Your Story.** Take a risk, set the tone and share your personal story with your students.

   **Springboard Questions:**
   - Where are you from?
   - Who are your people?
   - What is your culture?
   - Who raised you?
   - Why did you become a teacher?
   - Why are you teaching this unit?
   - What does reconciliation mean to you?

2. **Interview Your Partner.** Have the students **interview** a classmate or school staff member. As a class, brainstorm ethical interview questions—

questions that don't lead and that are open-ended and respectful (see Handout #4). Skills learned: formulating thoughtful questions, speaking, recording, synthesizing, representing.

3. **The Puzzle of Us.** Create an interactive biographical **Story Map.** This is a narrative map that shows locations marked by each class member's story. If your class has the resources, create a digital narrative map: storymap.knightlab. com. Or, using collage, you can also create a visual map. On a large piece of paper, draw and then cut out a puzzle. Hand out the pieces. The students have to create a biographical "puzzle piece" about the person they interviewed, using their interview questions.

4. **Learning through Ceremony.** Have each student introduce their classmate or school member and place their puzzle piece on the wall, until you have a complete puzzle. Emphasize that it is the **different** pieces that make the whole, and the whole is stronger than an isolated piece. Emphasize that each person must be **included** in order to complete the puzzle. Make the connection that studying Canada's history is, in part, investigating whose puzzle pieces (stories) are missing in Canada's mosaic.

5. **Create an "I am" Poem** (see Handout #5).

### Keep It Simple: What's in a Name?

**Create a Word Cloud** with just the names of the students in your class and the meaning of their birth names. Use a word-cloud tool and print the image for your room. You can also do this manually once the children have researched the origin of their name(s). Emphasize how our names are our first connections to our identity, our sense of self and our connectedness to others. Digital Word Cloud Resource: tagxedo.com.

## Learning Activity: Culture Clash

### Essential Questions:

- What are the differences between the Indigenous ways of being and learning and Western colonial approaches to education?
- How are language and culture connected?
- What values underpin colonialism?

*Teacher Instructions*

1. **Introduce the concept to your students:** Words speak to the mind; images speak to the heart. We are going to create a juxtaposition that speaks from both the mind and the heart.

2. **Start with the guiding question:** How do the values represented in the primary documents of Residential Schools in Canada contradict the "First Peoples' Principles of Learning"?

3. Have students **select a word**, quote or phrase from the book (or another print source) that speaks to them. Juxtapose it with a photograph or an image that also speaks to them.

4. In the "space between," have students **write a brief** comment about the message of their juxtaposition. Start with the stem "My juxtaposition speaks to the idea/question/feeling that…"

5. **Share** the juxtapositions in small groups.

*Student Instructions*

1. **Research** the nine "First Peoples' Principles of Learning." See: https://firstpeoplesprinciplesoflearning.wordpress.com/first-peoples-principles-of-learning.

2. **Essential Questions:**
   - What schoolwide practices already acknowledge some of these principles?
   - Based on these principles, what are some fundamental or universal conditions for learning?

3. **Interpreting Primary Documents:** Study the primary documents (photos) in chapter two. Most of these photos were staged to promote Residential Schools. When looking at archival photos, it is important to look at the photos as a sociologist.

4. **Questions for Discussion:**
   - What can you *not* see in the photos?
   - What do the faces tell you?
   - What is the tone and energy of the photos?
   - What does the body language say? What values about schooling are depicted in these photos?
   - What do the documents tell us about the purpose of colonization and the purpose of Residential Schools?

5. **Create a Juxtaposition:** A juxtaposition is two contradictory or opposing images that tell a different story when they are placed side by side. You can also juxtapose text with images.

## Learning Activity: Land as Witness

*Teacher Instructions*

Find a landmark in your neighbourhood that honours, either historically or artistically, the First Peoples of your area. Take a trip or show a photo of the landmark or monument. What does the site say about the relationships between the First Peoples and the land or the water, or with the settlers of the land?

*Student Instructions*

1. **Write a** third-person **poem** or a personification poem from the vantage point of the landmark or the land. What has this land witnessed?
2. **Write a letter** to your local government from the point of view of the land/water. What might our natural environment and resources say to the humans governing them right now?
3. **Read** the poem "Love Letter to the Land" by Wade Vaneltsi (see Handout #6).
4. **Write** a "sense poem" (see Handout #7) from the perspective of the landmark you discovered.
5. **Take a photo** of the natural area around your school. It could be a photo of the outline of winter branches against the blue sky. Create a written or spoken-word poem from the perspective of the photo. What are the messages and teachings of the natural world around you?
6. **Read** Tasha's interview with Wade on Handout #6. What are the possibilities and limitations of reconciliation?

TASHA HENRY

TASHA HENRY

13

## Learning Activity: Resilience and the Power of One

*Teacher Instructions*

1. **Watch** "The Stranger," the first music-video chapter of Gord Downie and Jeff Lemire's project *The Secret Path*: youtube.com/watch?v=za2VzjkwtFc. You can review the subsequent chapters to see if they are suitable for your age group. The piece may be painful to watch. Skip ahead to 46:00 and watch the section that interviews Chanie Wenjack's sisters: youtube.com/watch?v=yGd764YU9yc.

2. **Making Connections through Discussion:** What does Gord Downie mean when he says Chanie Wenjack is "the symbol"? What messages of resilience and strength are depicted in the book *When We Were Alone* and in the testimonies of Chanie's sisters?

*Student Instructions*

1. **Watch** the Tedx talk "Resilience and the Power of One" by Monique Gray Smith: youtube.com/watch?v=edMcljKndEQ.

2. **Study** "The Umbrella of Indigenous Resiliency" (see Handout #8) or review page 32.

3. **Read the storybook** *When We Were Alone*, written by David Alexander Robertson and illustrated by Julie Flett.

4. **Watch** "Tuesday Teaching from Boys with Braids" by Toyacoyah Brown: powwows.com/tuesday-teaching-boys-braids.

5. **Write a first-person letter** from the perspective of a person from a specific point in Canada's history. Use the umbrella handout for reference (see Handout #8). Using letter-writing conventions, consider writing to elected representatives from a specific time in history, like Duncan Campbell Scott. Then refer to Handout #11.

## Learning Activity: Learning to Listen as an Ethical Responsibility

*Teacher Instructions*

1. In groups, have students **explore** the "Reclaiming History Timeline" from the digital exhibit *Where are the Children*: http://wherearethechildren.ca/en/timeline.

2. **Review or role-play** the "Listening Respectfully" handout #4 on page 31.

3. **Preview** Residential School Survivors' stories and have the children view a whole testimony. Don't have them take notes while listening. Instead, explain to them the importance of being present when listening to testimony. Afterward, have them respond to the question: Why is listening to testimony with intention a Call to Action?

SHARI NAKAGAWA

4. **Create a Fact Box**: After studying the timeline from *Where are the Children?* have each student pick out a key event (or assign a key event by picking one from a bowl) and research the history of that particular event.

*Student Instructions*

1. **Essential Question:** What was the cause and effect of this key event in history?
2. On one side of a large index card, document the event. On the reverse side, describe the impact on Indigenous communities in Canada.
3. On the back of the index cards, number the events chronologically.
4. Decorate a shoebox or other type of box. Place all the index cards in the box. You can pull a card at random or use the cards sequentially. Can anyone place all the cards in sequential order without looking at the numbers?
5. Use the Fact Box throughout the unit to discuss how these points in history are still affecting current living conditions for Indigenous people.

## Learning Activity: Understanding Resistance

*Student Instructions*

1. **Read** the excerpt on page 77 about Dr. Bryce. How are communities and individuals defining resistance to colonialism?

2. **Watch** *Stadium Pow Wow* by A Tribe Called Red: youtube.com/watch?v=eA EmjW9J3_o&list=RDeAEmjW9J3_o#t=9.

3. **Essential Questions:**
   - What is the symbolism of the footage of the Hudson's Bay?
   - When you listen to the mix, what words come to mind about the message this band is sending to youth?
   - What is the cultural significance of the Pow Wow?

4. **Read** Kelsey Leonard's poem "Ribbon Skirt" (see Handout #10) aloud, alternating speakers. Try having it read by only female readers.

5. **Watch the video** on CBC's *Unreserved* called "Skirt Teachings with Myra Laramee": cbc.ca/radio/unreserved/videos-tuesday-teachings-1.4189868.

6. **Write a compare and contrast essay:** How would you describe the different ways that resistance is taken up by these artists?

7. **Possible thesis:** In the music video *Stadium Pow Wow* by A Tribe Called Red and the poem "Ribbon Skirt" by Kelsey Leonard, the ideas of cultural resistance are taken up using contrasting imagery.

## Culminating Learning Activity: Making Conceptual Art

*Student Instructions*

**Make Conceptual Art:** Create a **Response Piece**, choosing a medium that speaks to you. Photograph, draw, paint or build an abstract response to this chapter with a full explanation of the concepts or feelings that your piece represents and what you hope it will communicate to others. Analyze the symbolism of your materials in relation to the content of this chapter. Consider using found objects such as recycled materials, Lego or artifacts to construct your conceptual response piece.

1. **Write a one-page Artist's Statement.** This should describe the project, what it is responding to and what it hopes to communicate to the public.

2. Have a **panel discussion** about the concepts explored in the response pieces. In groups of four, answer questions from your peers and teachers about your work.

3. **Host** an art opening and invite guests.

4. **Document** your process and your final art by submitting your project to the Project of Heart: http://projectofheart.ca.

5.  Consider destroying the art pieces in a ceremony. Investigate this concept in relation to cultural traditions by studying the work of Beau Dick: http://vancouversun.com/news/staff-blogs/kwakwakawakw-potlatch-masks-art-made-to-be-destroyed.

**Keep It Simple**

*Student Instructions*

1.  **Create a poster**: Choose a province or territory in Canada. Research the First Peoples of that province/territory. Identify the languages and regions within the province/territory. Create a poster that poses a question to the people who live in that province about their commitment to reconciliation. View this project for inspiration: http://graphichistorycollective.com/project/remember-resist-redraw-poster-0-introduction.

2.  **Create a playlist or podcast** with musical contributions that explore the history of resistance and resilience through music. Develop an annotated bibliography of each music piece that explains your reasons for selecting each piece. Post your playlist on a music-sharing platform. Write an online "review" for a classmate's playlist.

SHARI NAKAGAWA

17

# CHAPTER THREE-LOVE: WHERE DO WE STAND TODAY?

## Summary

This chapter summarizes the recent national initiatives for redress in Canada and the history of the TRC. Reconciliation is defined as an ongoing process that requires personal, professional and institutional commitments to change. Love is emphasized as the binding force that enables positive change for all people.

## Essential Questions

- What are the criticisms of reconciliation?
- What are the possibilities and limitations of this work?

## Key Concepts and Vocabulary

the need for redress or reconciliation

social justice

barriers to justice

justice as an ongoing effort

honourary witness

94 Calls to Action

Indian Residential Schools Settlement Agreement (IRSSA)

Indian Residential Schools Survivor Committee (IRSSC)

national TRC events

National Centre for Truth and Reconciliation (NCTR)

Truth and Reconciliation Commision of Canada (TRC)

## Learning Activity: Researching Canada's TRC

1. *Entrance Slip:* Create or draw a Word Cloud in a shape that represents your reactions, comments and questions about chapter two using the tool at wordle.net.

2. **Create** a concrete poem that depicts an image of resiliency through the repetition of the word.

## Learning Activity: Background Biographical Research

*Student Instructions*

1. **Group work:** Who were the three Truth and Reconciliation commissioners?

2. **In small groups**, create a timeline for each commissioner, including key personal and professional accomplishments, a brief biography, two significant quotes from each person and three images. Give the members of your group research roles.

3. **Read** pages 87-88. Respond to the Reflection Questions. Have you been in situations where an apology wasn't enough?

4. **Define** *reconciliation* from the TRC document. Define it in your own words using simple language. What does it mean for you in terms of your social interactions?

5. **Questions to investigate:** Why do you think the Calls to Action are not merely recommendations? Which ones can your class address?

6. **Research** the seven National TRC Events outlined on pages 92-93.
   a) With a partner, create a flyer that identifies the events, speakers and theme of one of the seven events.
   b) Pin the flyers to a map of Canada for others to review.

**Learning Activity: Honourary Witnesses**
*Teacher Instructions*

## Research Jigsaw

1. **Read** together the section about honourary witnesses on page 94.

2. Split the class into groups of at least four. This is their "home group." Assign each person in each group a number from one to four. Give each home group the biography of one honourary witness from the TRC website: trc.ca/websites/reconciliation/index.php?p=331.

3. In the home group, the children **discuss** their honourary witness, and each student writes a small biography identifying the accomplishments and commitment that this witness has demonstrated. Large index cards work well.

4. **Break into numbered groups.** All the ones sit together, all the twos together, et cetera. Each person shares or reads the biographical information about their honourary witness. By the end of the jigsaw, each numbered group should have learned about three other people.

5. As a whole class, **develop a criteria** based on your research that identifies the qualities, attitudes and behaviours an honourary witness must possess.

**Learning Activity: Beyond Reconciliation**
After reading the chapter together, discuss what roadblocks you anticipate will arise on this journey to reconciliation.

1. **Watch** Chief Dr. Robert Joseph: youtube.com/watch?v=L6LkNAR44mI (parts one and two).

2. **Watch** *Healing a Nation Through Truth and Reconciliation* by Chief Dr. Robert Joseph: youtube.com/watch?v=rJQgpuLq1LI.

## Defining the Concept: Thinking through Graphic Organizers

*Teacher Instructions*

1. **Frayer Model**: Ask each student to fold a piece of paper in quarters (half and then half again).

2. Have them fold down a little triangle in the centre, where the four corners meet, so there is a diamond in the middle when they open it.

3. Ask students to write the word *reconciliation* in the diamond. They will then label the four quadrants *looks like, feels like, is not, shouldn't*.

4. In pairs or individually, have students list words or phrases that connect to each quadrant.

5. Have different students write the responses on four large pieces of poster board. Post in the classroom. Have the students do a gallery tour and read each other's thoughts, or have some students read from each poster board.

6. As a whole class, brainstorm a **simple KWL Chart** (What I *Know*, What I *Want* to Know, What I *Learned*).

7. In pairs or small groups, students will respond to the questions on page 76 with a graphic organizer (Mind Map or Flow Chart).

8. Students will complete the Extended KWL Grid (see Handout #9), either individually or with partners.

## Culminating Learning Activity: Committing to the Journey

**Create a reconciliation event:** This could be an afternoon event in a classroom, a school-based event or an ongoing community-engaged project. It doesn't have to be big—but it does have to be sincere! Try a community weave, a wish tree, a monthly oral storytelling event or an after-school sharing circle with outside community members. Who would be invited to this event? Over what period of time?

*Student Instructions*

## Brainstorm—3-2-1

1. In groups of three, **list 3 facts**, collaborate to come up with **2 questions** and develop **1 idea** around a community event that could be the beginning of reconciliation in your school.

2. In your groups, create criteria for an achievable event. Vote on the ideas as a class. Create a timeline. Delegate responsibilities. Sign a commitment contract.

3. Think about organizing a reconciliation event. Have a look at the Reconciliation Tool Kit website: bcasw.org/wp-content/uploads/2011/06/Reconciliation-Toolkit-Final_May-11.pdf

# CHAPTER FOUR-KINDNESS AND RECIPROCITY: WHERE DO WE GO FROM HERE?

## Summary

This chapter explores the attitudes and dispositions needed to create social change. Values and beliefs are explored by examining agency, citizenship, voice, action and what it means to be an ally. Students are encouraged to investigate their own privilege, citizenship and advocacy by researching initiatives and projects that support social justice and positive change for Indigenous and non-Indigenous relations.

## Key Concepts and Vocabulary

ally
genocide
privilege
reciprocity

## Metaphors for Learning:

building bridges, land-based learning, love

## Essential Questions

- How is reciprocity integral to the ongoing process of reconciliation?
- What does reciprocity look like societally?
- What does it look like institutionally?

## Learning Activity: Check Your Privilege

*Entrance Slip:* Whose words are with you today? Are you feeling hopeful? Or discouraged? Why?

## Learning Activity: Social Experiment

*Teacher Instructions*

1. Put a recycling bin at the front of the class.
2. Instruct students to scrunch up three pieces of paper each. They will each get to throw the balls of paper into the recycling bin from their desks. Whoever gets all three in won't have to write one assignment.
3. Tell them to start. If they protest that it's not fair, tell them that that's not really your concern.
4. After the paper toss, have them discuss what it was like to be at the back of the class. What did you feel? How were you feeling when you were at

the front of the class? When you are the one privileged, are you thinking about the disadvantaged? Do you see your privilege? Discuss how privilege is something that is not earned: it is just given or inherited.

### Learning Activity: Respect Is a Verb—Moving from Words to Actions
*Student Instructions*

1. **Listen** to the keynote talk by Senator Murray Sinclair on the podcast *Red Man Laughing*, outlined on page 99. Go to 49:38 in the podcast.

2. **Listening Responses:** What three dispositions does he reference as key to the healing process for Myrtle and John?

3. **Questions for Discussion:** What actions signify mutual respect between Indigenous and non-Indigenous people in your community? How can self-respect be returned to Survivors of Residential Schools? What actions beyond emotions such as empathy are needed?

4. **Activity:** Words that Stay with Me. Pick five quotes from the entire unit or from *Speaking Our Truth*. Write each quote on the front of a small index card. On the reverse, choose a writing stem to describe why you picked this quote:

   This quote reminds me to…

   This quote challenges me to…

   This quote inspires me to…

5. **Inspiration Jar:** Keep the cards in a jar or basket. Each day throughout the rest of the year, someone can draw a quote to read to the class.

### Learning Activity: Claiming the Calls to Action
*Student Instructions*

1. **Review** the Calls to Action. As a class, decide which call seems attainable in terms of available resources, time and budget. Create a proposal with a timeline and submit it to your school administration. Delegate responsibilities.

2. As a class, **decide** what parts of the social interactions within your school need positive attention. Define what attitudes need a collective call to action in terms of social interactions. Define five calls that are simply worded and achievable for your age group. Submit these calls to your school principal as a potential addition to your school's Code of Conduct.

3. Does your school have a traditional territory acknowledgment? In the foyer? On its website? **Host a design contest.** The winning emblem or symbol should represent kindness, respect and reciprocity within your school. The winning image could be used for the school letterhead.

4. **Cover a bulletin board** with your territory acknowledgment, your homage to Survivors and samples of your work in this unit to promote positive relationships in your school community.

5. **Develop a proposal** that responds to one or some of the Calls to Action. What are the positive behaviours that can be practiced on a daily level? What space is there for daily acknowledgments? In the morning announcements?

6. **Start a column** in the monthly school newsletter that focuses on six initiatives or interventions for six months.

## Learning Activity: Creating a Learning Resource
*Student Instructions*

Look back at the interview you conducted in the first chapter. Using the questions Monique developed to create this book, interview the same person again.

Monique's Interview Questions:
1. What have you learned about Residential Schools at home?
2. What have you learned about Residential Schools at school?
3. What do you hope for our country?

## Culminating Activity: Re-Visioning Canada
*Student Instructions*

The Ministry of Immigration, Refugees and Citizenship has mandated that the swearing-in oath for new citizens must reflect an oath to honour Indigenous treaties. New Canadians will be given a package that prepares them for this oath taking. As a class, decide what activities and assignments you feel new Canadians must understand and participate in before they take this oath. Analyze this quote from Senator Murray Sinclair as you consider what guidance new Canadians need to advocate for positive change for Indigenous communities: "It's not just about the wording of an oath. It's about ensuring that those who are coming to live in this country permanently in the future are also well-informed, so when they do take the oath, it has more meaning for them" (CBC interview, Feb. 2, 2017).

1. **Read** "New Canadians to pledge honour for Indigenous Treaties in revised citizenship oath" (from CBC News/Politics, Feb. 2, 2017: http://cbc.ca/news/politics/citizenship-oath-indigenous-treaties-1.3963508).

2. **Brainstorm** a table of contents for a "New Canadians" package. Each group takes one section of the table of contents.

3. **Each group creates a poster** or a brochure that is designed to educate new Canadian children and youth about Indigenous history in Canada. This tool may help students who have access to technology: postermywall.com/index.php/posterbuilder.

4. **Research** the current swearing-in oath and modify it to honour Indigenous treaties. Send your proposal/brochure to Prime Minister Trudeau.

## Closing Interview Juxtaposition

*Student Instructions*

1. **Juxtapose** your initial interview with the closing interview.
2. Pick three entries from this entire unit that show your best thinking and your best work. Edit and polish your work so that it is ready to publish.
3. **Create** a Learning Resource for your school library. It could be in the form of a scrapbook, portfolio, anthology or electronic file (ebook, blog, etc.).
4. **Write** an introduction that guides new teachers into the "do's and dont's" of this curriculum from a learner's perspective.
5. **Contact** other schools in your district. Would those teachers like a copy? Could you meet with other classes and share your work? Could you teach a small lesson to a younger grade? Would the Native Friendship Centre in your city or town like a copy?

**Keep It Simple**

Close the unit with a final reflection. Upload a personal reflection, called a "Personal Ribbon" or "Twibbon," on the TRC "It Matters to Me" website: trc.ca/websites/reconciliation/index.php?p=328.

## Curriculum Extensions: Artist as Activist

**Essential Questions:**

- What questions are being asked by contemporary Indigenous artists?
- What social and political issues are artists challenging through their art?

*Student Instructions*

1. **Question for Discussion/Research:** What other forms of protest, either local or international, are rooted in the idea that the First Peoples are our "land protectors"?
2. **Study** the work of the two artists below, or choose two other contemporary Indigenous artists.
   - Andy Everson's "Star Wars" series.
   - Christi Belcourt's project *Walking With Our Sisters*: http://christibelcourt.com/walking-with-our-sisters.
3. **Project Proposal:** Using specific reference to the cultural significance of their work, explain how each artist could be described as a cultural warrior.

**Tasha Henry** has been travelling, writing and teaching for the past twenty years. She is a published writer and poet and holds a Master of Education in Language, Culture and Teaching from York University. She has taught high-school students and has trained teachers across Canada as well as internationally. She currently lives on unceded Lekwungen territory in Victoria, British Columbia.

TASHA HENRY

# HANDOUTS

As a classroom teacher you may reproduce the materials in this book for use in a single classroom only. The reproduction of any part of this book for other classrooms or for an entire school or school system is strictly prohibited.

Name:_____

Dear Parent(s)/Guardian(s),

As part of our (Social Studies/Language Arts) curriculum, in the coming weeks we will be starting a unit about Canada's relationship with Indigenous peoples through the concept of reconciliation.

We have created age-appropriate and culturally sensitive lessons and activities that will explore the impacts of colonialism in Canadian history, including Residential Schooling, using the book *Speaking Our Truth: A Journey of Reconciliation*, by Monique Gray Smith.

This subject is difficult to teach, and we are aware that the content may trigger intergenerational trauma for our First Nations, Métis and Inuit families. We want you to be aware that conversations may emerge in the home around this topic, and we encourage you to join the conversation and support the journey of reconciliation with us.

If you have any questions or concerns, please feel free to contact us at any time.

Warmly,
(Teachers)

Entrance Slip: One question I have today is…

Exit Slip: One thing that struck me was…

One thing I want to ask/share with my teacher is…

| Topic | Watching / Listening | Analyzing Primary Documents | Reading Secondary Sources | Experiencing Guests/Out-trips |
|---|---|---|---|---|
| Indigenous Ways of Knowing | (video) *Symbolism of the Eagle Feather* (Adrian LaChance) | Artifacts: Regalia, Feather, Drum (presented by Chief Ron George) | • Medicine Wheel handout<br>• Seven Sacred Teachings | • Smudging<br>• Lindsay Delaronde (Mohawk/Iroquois) beading on moosehide |
| Canada's Indian Act | (video) *CAP—On Canada's Indian Act* (Patrick Brazeau)<br>*Toronto Star*: Shareable Facts | • Indian Act 1886 and 1894<br>• Historical excerpts | (website) Government of Canada "Indian Act and Justice Laws" | |
| Colonialism and Eurocentrism | | • Art in textbooks<br>• Map of colonialism | "Colonial Clash" handout (FNESC) | • Honouring Songhees territory<br>• Songhees Wellness Centre |
| Cultural Stereotyping | (video) *I'm Not the Indian You Had in Mind* (Thomas King) | Textbooks (art depicting stereotyping) | Craig Kielburger's interview with Thomas King (handout) | |
| Residential Schools | Reading of *Shi Shi Etko*: youtube.com/watch?v=e7HXqTaLkLE | • Map work<br>• Photo of Kuper Island school and floor plan<br>• School-food letters | • Kuper Island story<br>• Kuper Island handout *When We Were Alone* and *Shi-shi-etko* storybooks | Ron Tsaskiy George, Hereditary Chief (Wet'suwet'en) |
| Cultural Resiliency | Tedx Talks: Monique Gray Smith "Resilience and the Power of One" | Photo analysis:<br>• Oka Crisis<br>• DAPL | • Umbrella of Indigenous Resiliency<br>• Four blankets | Monique Gray Smith reading *Tilly* |
| Oral History | CBC: Roy Henry Vickers tells the story of the Orca Chief | (audio) *Cloud Walker* (R.H. Vickers) | (audio/video) Leanne Betasamosake Simpson | • Lucky Budd: Oral-history expert<br>• Butch Dick |
| First Nations Traditional and Contemporary Art | | Carvings Art Thompson & Hjalmer Wenstob | | • Lekwungen Spindle Whorls walking tour<br>• Richard Hunt<br>• Nicholas Galanin |

**Handout #3**
**Learning Grid:**
**Identifying the**
**Ways We Learn**

②

Name:_____

| Last lesson, I learned… | Today we learned… | Feelings/thoughts I have… |
|---|---|---|
| What I don't understand is… | My burning question is… | I hope that… |

## Handout #4
## Listening Respectfully

Name: _____

Monique likes to say, "We have one mouth and two ears for a reason." As you begin this work, let's practice ways of listening respectfully and ethically to others when they are sharing their stories and truths.

1. Sit across from a partner and have them talk about their past weekend (what they did, who they saw). Ask them to speak in their first language, even if it is different from yours.

2. As you listen, notice your body language. Are your arms crossed?

3. Try having your shoulders face your partner. Place your hands in a neutral position (folded, clasped but not clenched).

4. Make eye contact.

5. Nod silently instead of inserting your voice.

6. Be present—imagine all of yourself intent on listening to your partner.

7. Be calm in your body so that they feel comfortable speaking to you.

8. When they have finished speaking, simply acknowledge with a "thank you."

9. Switch roles.

10. Give constructive feedback to each other. At which point did you feel your partner was practicing "deep listening"?

Orca Book Publisher © 2018 *Speaking Our Truth: A Journey of Reconciliation* Teacher Guide by Tasha Henry • ISBN 9781459822221

## Handout #5
## I Am...

Name:_____

A Poem by _____  Grade_____

### *Writing Stems*

Complete each stem with a word or a phrase. You can also leave the "I am" lines blank for impact! Do you speak another language? Consider infusing your stems with vocabulary from your language. Don't forget to add your choice of punctuation at the end of each line!

I am _____

I am looking at/for _____

I am learning to _____

I am listening to _____

I am remembering _____

I used to _____

I am _____

I am waiting for _____

I am running on/with _____

I am chasing _____

I am hoping _____

I am living _____

I am _____

Name:_____

**"A Love Letter to the Land"** by Wade Clifford Vaneltsi

The land is always showing us and teaching us the ways of life.
The land and animals are always reminding us how to live.
The trees remind us to stand tall and to be patient.
The grass reminds us to be persistent.
The fire reminds us that we are stronger when united.
The water reminds us to be open and accepting to the diversity in this world.
The wind reminds us that our voice can travel great distances.
The earth reminds us in many ways that we came from it and that we will return to
    it when we walk on from this life.
The caribou reminds us to unite as a nation of pride.
The wolf reminds us to love and protect our family.
The raven reminds us to be creative.
The wolverine reminds us to be resilient and always aware.
The beaver reminds us to always conserve.
The fish reminds us to be transformative.
The bear reminds us to embody the spirit we all have inside.
Our land and our animals are out there, waiting to teach us these important values
    of life.
They depend on us just as much as we depend on them.
They come together in harmony to deliver us a message that we all need to hear. If
    you look deep into our land, you will begin to understand everything in a way
    you cannot imagine.
You will see and feel life in moments that will ignite the spirit within you,
and if you breathe and embrace the golden silence of our land you will realize that
    it has a song for those who listen,
a song of love.

## Questions for Discussion

1. In Wade's poem, he talks about how animals instruct his knowledge. Do you
   think Canada's First Peoples view animals differently than other cultures?
2. What is the difference between hearing and listening?
3. How would you describe Wade's relationship to the land?
4. If the land had a message to youth, what would it be?
5. If you were to write a letter to Prime Minister Trudeau or your local MLA from
   the point of view of the land, what would you request? Be specific—write from
   the perspective of a specific river, forest, valley, etc.

Orca Book Publisher © 2018 *Speaking Our Truth: A Journey of Reconciliation* Teacher Guide by Tasha Henry • ISBN 9781459822221

## Tasha's Interview with Wade

1. **Where are you from?** I am from the community of Tetlit Zheh (Fort McPherson), Northwest Territories.

2. **Who are your people?** My people are the Tetlit Gwich'in First Nations (the Mountain People).

3. **What does your name mean?** I have a traditional name, Zhóh Zraii, which means "Black Wolf" in the Tetlit Gwich'in dialect. I've yet to find out if my last name holds any meaning, as a lot of families in the north had their last names modernized during the Residential Schools era as part of the colonial assimilation agenda.

4. **When did you start writing poetry?** I only started in June 2016 and have only written a few poems. I've been working on music lately and am looking to record an album soon with a singer I'm working with.

5. **In your poem, you talk about what animals teach you. Do you think Indigenous peoples view animals differently than other cultures do?** I believe that all Indigenous cultures around the world learn from the animals of their homeland the same way my people have learned from the animals on our homeland. Every animal on this planet has a lesson to teach us, and I think we have to re-establish our relationship with them to find out what they want to pass on to us.

6. **What is the difference between hearing and listening?** It's kind of hard to answer, but I think most people are hearing their surroundings in their daily commutes, but to listen to one person or thing out of everything you're hearing is to submit yourself to the lesson or message that this one thing/person has for you.

7. **What is your relationship to the land?** The land is my culture; the land teaches me, feeds me, gives me shelter and sometimes blessings.

8. **If the land had a message to youth, what would it be?** I think the message would be, "Let us reconnect."

9. **What does reconciliation mean to you?** It doesn't mean much to me when it comes to how Canada's government goes about its reconciling with First Nations and all other nations across the country. The government thinks that by [their] simply apologizing, we could just move on from the cultural genocide and assimilation they implemented on our people. Giving money to [Residential School Survivors] only makes things worse. Most of the Survivors didn't accept the money, as it doesn't fix the damage that has been done to the spirit, the land, the people and the culture. To reconcile is to harmonize, but it doesn't seem to be happening just yet.

10. **If you were to write a letter to Prime Minister Trudeau from the point of view of the land or water, what would you ask for?** I would demand that the government and Crown give back the lands they confiscated from us, and I would ask for equity when it comes to the starvation wages we are given to care for our people in our small communities.

**Sense Poem** by Wade Clifford Vaneltsi

**I hear** the ongoing madness of technology and vehicles, but I also hear the Elder drumming and singing on his steps.

**I see** a jet flying high above but the Eagle I also see, owns the sky.

**I taste** the colonial food but it doesn't taste as good as my caribou or geese would.

**I smell** the pollution that's slowly making its way into our lands but I also smell the smoke of the fire I feed.

**I feel** the weight of the responsibility that has been passed on to me, but I also feel ready for the tasks that come with the responsibility.

**I know** my ancestors live on through these responsibilities that have been passed down to each generation, their blood still flows strong.

**I know** this because the land is still here, and our animals are still here, and because of my ancestors,

**I'm here.**

Orca Book Publisher © 2018 *Speaking Our Truth: A Journey of Reconciliation* Teacher Guide by Tasha Henry • ISBN 9781459822221

Create a Sense Poem from the point of view of the land/water or an animal/ bird in your region.

**I am** (name of geographical location/animal)_____

**I hear** _____

_____

**I see** _____

_____

**I taste** _____

_____

**I smell** _____

_____

**I feel** _____

_____

**I know** _____

_____

**I am here.**

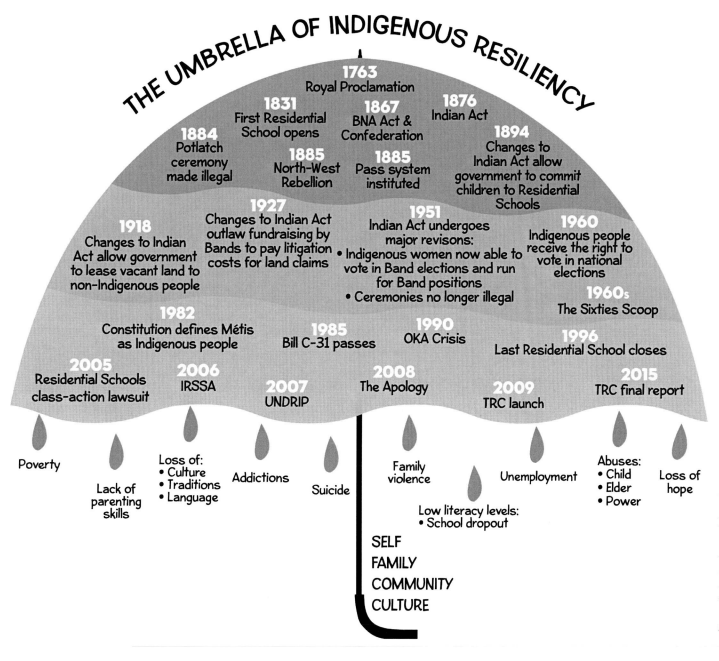

## THE UMBRELLA OF INDIGENOUS RESILIENCY

**1763**
Royal Proclamation

**1831**
First Residential
School opens

**1867**
BNA Act &
Confederation

**1876**
Indian Act

**1884**
Potlatch
ceremony
made illegal

**1885**
North-West
Rebellion

**1885**
Pass system
instituted

**1894**
Changes to
Indian Act allow
government to commit
children to Residential
Schools

**1918**
Changes to Indian
Act allow government
to lease vacant land to
non-Indigenous people

**1927**
Changes to Indian Act
outlaw fundraising by
Bands to pay litigation
costs for land claims

**1951**
Indian Act undergoes
major revisons:
• Indigenous women now able to
vote in Band elections and run
for Band positions
• Ceremonies no longer illegal

**1960**
Indigenous people
receive the right to
vote in national
elections

**1960s**
The Sixties Scoop

**1982**
Constitution defines Métis
as Indigenous people

**1985**
Bill C-31 passes

**1990**
OKA Crisis

**1996**
Last Residential School closes

**2005**
Residential Schools
class-action lawsuit

**2006**
IRSSA

**2007**
UNDRIP

**2008**
The Apology

**2009**
TRC launch

**2015**
TRC final report

Poverty

Lack of
parenting
skills

Loss of:
• Culture
• Traditions
• Language

Addictions

Suicide

Family
violence

Low literacy levels:
• School dropout

Unemployment

Abuses:
• Child
• Elder
• Power

Loss of
hope

SELF

FAMILY

COMMUNITY

CULTURE

Orca Book Publisher © 2018 *Speaking Our Truth: A Journey of Reconciliation Teacher Guide* by Tasha Henry • ISBN 9781459822221

# Handout #9
## Extended KWL Chart

Name:_____

| I knew… | I now know… | I want to know… |
|---|---|---|
| | | |

| I used to feel… | I now feel… | My hope is… |
|---|---|---|
| | | |

| I used to wish… | I now wish… | My baby step is… |
|---|---|---|
| | | |

| I used to say… | Now I will say… | My actions will say… |
|---|---|---|
| | | |

**"Ribbon Skirt"** by Kelsey Leonard

I wear you to pray
For humility
For Power
In the sway of my skirt
I can feel my ancestors tug
Gentle resurgence of love
Carrying millennia of tradition in each step
keenly aware of the way
this imperial cloth brushes my thighs
Yet balanced with the vibrancy of my ribbons
cut, ironed and sewn just right to breathe
Indigenous knowledge into my existence
so when the other looks at me
They look confused
But still I stand
Humble in prayer
in Power
in Resistance
Building waves of survivance
With my sway
So that my babies unborn are awakened in a world that claims
Their spiritual existence
And on the days when I am tired and weak
My sway
soothes my weary soul
And reminds me that
I am descended from warriors
I am a carrier of tradition
And am their living breath eternal
with each sway of my step
I am Love.

Orca Book Publisher © 2018 *Speaking Our Truth: A Journey of Reconciliation Teacher Guide by Tasha Henry* • ISBN 9781459822221

## Written/Oral Responses

1. How is the ribbon skirt a symbol of Kelsey's connection to her culture?
2. How is her skirt a symbol of Indigenous connection to the land and water?
3. What is the significance of regalia in First Nations, Métis and Inuit cultures?
4. How does Kelsey redefine resistance through her imagery of her ribbon skirt?
5. What gives you strength on tough days?

## Visual Response

Draw a picture of a piece of clothing, regalia, accessory (watch, knife, ring, etc.) or family treasure that has been passed down to you that has sentimental or cultural meaning. What does this object represent to you?

## Tasha's interview with Kelsey

1. **If the land or water had a message to youth, what would it be?** The land and water remembers. It is our relative. It cares for us. Tell it your thoughts, hopes, dreams and prayers. The land and water will pass those hopes, dreams and prayers on to future generations. It connects across time and reminds us that we are one strand in the greater web of life. We are not alone. We are still here. We are resilient.

2. **What does reconciliation mean to you?** An Elder said to me once, "There are many, many things that they told us about this time." They said that "at this time you would see young people with old spirits." They said, "You are going to see healers—the red, the yellow, the black and the white—and that each healer is given a talent and a gift. Some are given the gift to write, some to talk, some to lead, some to do art. Each one would have a gift." They said that "no gift alone could do it, no gift by itself could heal the peoples of the earth. But all the gifts together could bring about that healing." For me, reconciliation is the realization of this prophecy that we begin to heal the land and water by healing ourselves. We recognize and find our unique gifts the creator has given each of us and work to collaborate with others in our global world to use those gifts collectively for the betterment of our communities.

3. **If you were to write a letter to Prime Minister Trudeau from the point of view of the land/water, what would you ask for?** I think, as nature, I would write the letter to all the leaders of the world's nation-states and tell them to listen to Indigenous peoples and to value Indigenous science and knowledge. These peoples, the river, ocean, tree, etc. are all my relatives. They have lived with me since time immemorial. They have adapted to my changes, and their knowledge is key to my protection for future generations.

**Sense Poem** by Kelsey Leonard

**I am** Shinnecock (People of the Shore)
**I hear** waves lapping
**I see** whales' tails offshore
**I taste** saltwater in the air
**I smell** sage, cedar, sweetgrass
**I feel** loved
**I know** we are resilient
**I am here.**

Lila Smith
Lejac Residential School
Fraser Lake, BC

November 18, 1930

My dear yat'se,

Lila, please understand. I didn't want to send you away to Lejac Residential School. I didn't realize they would be coming for you so soon. I wasn't prepared for them to take you. I feel guilty for letting them take you, but the government says that this education will provide you with many opportunities and I had no choice. I think English will be useful, and your Abba and I cannot teach you how to write in English. But Lila, the school will make you think that the ways of the Nadleh Whut'en are wrong. The Roman Catholic ways are not better, just different. Practice everything that your Elders have taught you. Remember how to smoke salmon and make tobacco offerings, and more importantly, remember our Dakelh language. Practice speaking our language with your friends so you can come home and be with us again soon.

I can't wait to see you again in *dayun*. When you return, the berries will be ripening and I will make a fresh *bedutleh*. We are so close but so far away. I cannot see your gorgeous brown eyes looking at me.

Love,
Aloo

Orca Book Publisher © 2018 *Speaking Our Truth: A Journey of Reconciliation Teacher Guide* by Tasha Henry • ISBN 9781459822221

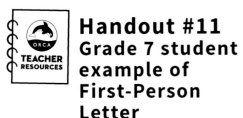

**Handout #11
Grade 7 student
example of
First-Person
Letter**

Name:_____

Indian Affairs Branch
Department of Health
Winnipeg, Manitoba

May 5, 1903

Dear Sir,

I am displeased to report that there have been some disturbances at the Kuper Island Residential School concerning the pupils. The Cowichan First Peoples have been complaining of improper treatment of the children, such as complaints of improper education, inadequate medical attention, lack of proper nutrition, and physical and emotional abuse. Not to mention the restrictions of speaking their native language, Hul'q'umi'num. I have addressed some of these problems with the headmaster of the school.

After further inspection of the school, I found that the school was not providing even the most basic needs of the pupils. When I arrived, none of the children were inside the building. They were working outside. Many seemed malnourished and looked quite sick and neglected. I also looked at the food supply and it was pathetic. Many of the children had not been fed. The spoiled food was still being used to make meals for the children.

As the assigned physician to the school, I find the state that the pupils are in is completely unacceptable. A new headmaster needs to be assigned immediately. I have released all the children back to their families, as the state they are being kept in is inhumane.

Please address the urgency of this situation.

Sincerely,
Dr. Peter Sampson